Copyright © 2010 by Larry Keltto and Jim Sheard, Ph.D.
Published by The Solopreneur Life Books
Owatonna, Minnesota
(507) 455-2136

ISBN-13: 978-0-615-44032-3
ISBN-10: 0615440320

RELATIONSHIP MARKETING
for
Solopreneurs:
How to Build Rewarding Connections in Work and Life

Larry Keltto and Jim Sheard, Ph.D.

The Solopreneur Life Books

CONTENTS

Introduction

Solopreneurs work on their own to establish and run an enterprise. The solopreneur may serve clients, customers, patrons (of a nonprofit), insured (an insurance agency or independent adjuster), or members (fitness centers). The list could go on to include the small retail store owner, the tradesperson (mechanic shop, plumber, lawn service), hair stylist, sales agent, multilevel marketer, personal trainer, attorney, financial planner, accountant, and many other forms of work that have been called "connectors."

There is a bit of the solopreneur spirit in all of us because, in a sense, we all work for ourselves. Ultimately we are responsible for our own connections, professional development, marketing, and how we treat others in relationships. The only difference is some get to be their "own boss" each day.

True solopreneurs are those who have

taken the plunge to be a solo worker and to determine their pay and satisfaction, based on what they are able to accomplish through their connections and personal productivity.

Relationship Marketing for Solopreneurs is for aspiring, new, and established solopreneurs who want to be successful at building rewarding relationships for work and life. It is about the skills needed to succeed in business, whether you have jumped into ownership or not.

Solopreneurs take responsibility for their relationships and career success—they are the ultimate self-empowered people.

— Jim Sheard, Ph.D.
September 2010

PART I

INITIATE CONNECTION

...TO HAVE AN OPPORTUNITY

Relationship marketing is the process of being in contact with people who have common interests, in order to create opportunities for rewarding connections to emerge.

Every relationship has a beginning. You can usually trace it back to the time when the relationship was first given a chance to develop. It may begin as a chance encounter, such as meeting a new member of your service organization, or it might be an intentional meeting with a prospective client. These are called "connections." They are the initial step in building a relationship.

To proactively seek connections, it helps to ask these three questions:

- What are my goals in my business and in life?
- How can relationships help me achieve those goals?
- Whom do I want to meet to continue to achieve those goals?

The truth is, you don't always know how a relationship will benefit you or the other person. The key is to connect in a way that gives the relationship an opportunity to grow and thrive.

Key #1

Know Your Goal

SUCCESS IN ANY BUSINESS REQUIRES CONNECTING WITH PEOPLE.

BE A FRIEND.

When developing goals for your business and your life, take it one step further and identify the specific people, or types of people, who are important for the achievement of your goals.

When the time is right, initiate contact with these individuals. If you see them as potential clients, be upfront about why you have reached out.

You have to make choices.

Connecting with people and striving to have them as clients is one of your primary business objectives. One of the biggest challenges in most solo businesses is finding enough work to be profitable.

Finding clients can seem like an all-consuming task. As much as you would like to make contact with dozens of people each day, time is limited.

So how do you choose?

Keep your business goals in mind and ask yourself how a particular contact fits with what you have set out to achieve.

Concentrate on strengthening your connection with the people you have identified. Never forget to make fun part of the equation. When choosing people with whom to connect, think about the ones you enjoy the most. Enjoyment is an indicator of how effective and productive a relationship will be. Also recognize that not everyone you serve in your business is going to become your best friend. Success for your business will involve working with all kinds of people.

**Relationships are not only
about your goals.**

Take joy and satisfaction from the fact that you can help others reach their goals. Consider which people would benefit the most from your time and attention, and give them priority.

Ask Yourself:

How many people will I need to connect with (as prospects) in order to make my business a success?

Think About It:

What are the primary ways I will make those connections?

Remember:

The strength of your relationships will determine whether you reach your goals.

Know Your Goal

"Thrivers seek to maximize their contribution. They have a clear sense of purpose."

— David McNally

"I went out to make friends and found none. I went out to be a friend and found many."

— Anonymous

"Relationships are essentially transactional. But the reality is that most of the greatest achievements and the greatest joys in life come through relationships that are transformational. In the very nature of the interaction, people are altered. They are transformed. Something new is created and neither person is controlling it. Neither could have anticipated it…It's a function of the exchange of understanding, insights, new learnings, and excitement around those new learnings."

— Stephen R. Covey

Take the Initiative

SOMEONE NEEDS TO TAKE THE FIRST STEP.

YOU CAN BE THAT PERSON.

You must be alert, open, and alive to possibilities for making connections.

The way in which you connect is the first impression you make on another person. A warm smile, a friendly greeting, and an upbeat conversation will open doors to relationships. The same is true when the first connection is online or on the phone.

Taking the initiative to meet another person is a risk that is often rewarded.

But miss the chance, and you will never know what could have come from the relationship.

Ways to take the initiative to connect:

Anticipate. Anticipate with whom, when, how, and where you will take the initiative.

Take a risk. The downside of not taking the initiative is missed opportunity.

Take responsibility. Your relationships are your responsibility.

Let go of fear. Your mind and your positive thoughts are in charge.

Persevere. It is not enough to take the initiative. Be friendly, warm, caring, and selfless. People will respond.

Be complimentary. If there are things you admire about someone else, let that person know.

In some situations, taking the initiative will be a face-to-face action. It might mean walking across a room at a meeting and introducing yourself to someone. Or, it might mean scheduling an appointment with a person who is new to your town. In a different setting it could mean writing an e-mail to another solopreneur and complimenting them on something they did.

In other situations, taking the initiative will be an action that you hope will attract potential clients. It will involve getting others to react in a way that creates a connection. For example, you may post a new offer on your Web site in order to move people to respond.

Ask Yourself:
When was the last time I took the first step to begin a relationship?

Think About It:
Initiating connections is important for my success and happiness.

Remember:
Relationships are the key to marketing my solo business.

Take the Initiative

*Connecting with people is the beginning of a
process that may lead to a relationship and a
venture of success and shared experiences.*
— Jim Sheard

*When you let go of your judgments and create
a moment of connection with another person,
you take the first step toward being truly
compassionate.*
— Barbara DeAngelis

*All human beings possess a desire to connect with
other people.*
— John Maxwell

Key # 3

Be Imaginative

Look for creative ways to connect with potential customers.

Be yourself.

Dare to put yourself "out there," in front your audience.

Every relationship begins with a first contact, and the universe of choices for making that initial connection has never been larger. Use your imagination to build a connection strategy. Create connection tools that people remember.

And know this: you can make a statement about your character and trustworthiness by following through on what you say you will do. Or, you can ruin your reputation by not being true to your word.

You never know where or how you will connect with your next client.

The important thing with all connection tools is this: be yourself. Trying to adopt a different persona is like being a theater performer: you can stay in character for a few hours, and the cheers from the audience are thrilling, but you cannot remain in character 24 hours a day, day after day, week after week.

If you want to be in business for years instead of months, put the "real you" in front of your audience.

Use your "voice."

Many of your connection messages will be in written form, and it's critical to write in a "voice" that matches who you are.

To do that, you must speak and write with honesty: express what you feel, share your opinions, and choose words that you actually use.

Remember, when a connection moves forward and becomes one-on-one, your customers or clients want to meet the person who matches the image they saw online, in a newspaper ad, or elsewhere.

Connection Tools

When selecting ways to reach your audience, align yourself with methods, symbols, organizations, and activities that are natural for you. For example, if you are a fan of cars and racing, then sponsoring a local race-car driver might be a great idea; you would be aligning yourself with people who share a common interest, which is the topic we will cover in Key #4.

Offline Tools

• **Logos**. Creating a logo as part of your brand is fundamental and critical for a comprehensive connection (and marketing) strategy.

• **Car signage.** As the number of solopreneurs has grown, so has the use of business signage on vehicles. Like many offline (and online) tools, though, its effectiveness is difficult to measure.

• **Billboards.** Not everyone can do it, but we

know a very successful real-estate agent who has based her marketing efforts over the past 15 years on the use billboards.

• **Promotional products.** The possibilities are limitless. Nearly every object can be stamped, engraved, or woven with your logo and used to create an impression.

• **Newsletters** are an ongoing way to touch your audience and establish your expertise.

• **Business cards** offer an important opportunity to express yourself and identify your business. Go online and search "cool business cards" to see the possibilities.

• **Community involvement.** Participating in clubs, sports leagues, fraternal organizations, religious groups, and other organizations puts you in the midst of business owners and leaders.

• **Donation** of products and services to charity auctions gives you visibility. In some communities of people, silent auctions are huge events. Be part of them.

• **Philanthropy.** Like community involvement, service to charitable organizations raises your profile among people you want to meet.

• **Association memberships.** Your field is likely to have trade and professional groups that offer multiple ways to connect with peers.

Online Tools

• **Web sites** are an absolute necessity for establishing connections. Sites give you a constant, worldwide presence.

• **Blogs.** If you write regularly and well for your blog, it can drive traffic to your Web site, boost your rankings in search engines, and give you a platform to establish your authority.

• **E-newsletters.** Delivered to your database list, e-newsletters are a tool for establishing, maintaining, or building relationships.

• **Social media.** This includes the current Big Three (Twitter, Facebook, and LinkedIn), plus membership-based, niched Web sites. Most of the niched, fee-based Web sites include discussion forums, which can be a tremendous way for you to share your knowledge and connect with people in your target market.

Audio and video. Once out of reach for many solopreneurs, audio and video now are viable options, thanks to the Internet. If these media are a good match for your talents and you can execute well, they can be influential in the marketplace.

Ask Yourself:
How can I express my personality through my connection methods?

Think About It:
Consistency in your messages is just as important as frequency.

Remember:
Candor and uniqueness are important "connectors."

When you innovate, you've got to be prepared for everyone telling you you're nuts.

— Larry Ellison

Key #4

Find Common Interests

RELATIONSHIPS BEGIN WITH
SOMETHING IN COMMON.

COMMON INTERESTS
FUEL CONNECTION.

Mutual interests open the door for getting to know someone.

Common interests bring people together; they make the initial connection possible. Finding and cultivating mutual interests is essential to a relationship. It is important to uncover the potential common ground and then do something to nurture it. Common interests can include nearly every activity and subject you can imagine. A few examples of broad subjects are: hobbies, sports, movies, TV, music, children, pets, schools that you attended, food, travel.

The challenge is to discover those common interests so that the initial connection can be explored. That is why you have to be imaginative and use a variety of media or tools to connect with people. Frankly, if there is no common interest then there is no reason to connect with someone. It sounds harsh, but it is true. Remember, too, that your business service and the other person's needs might be the common interest.

A shared acquaintance is a common interest.

One common interest is when you know someone in common. A friend of ours makes a hobby of seeking to find out who he and new acquaintances know in common. Once he finds that commonality, it opens up the conversation to topics related to that acquaintance and soon he has a "new friend."

Larry played golf recently with a new

acquaintance. They quickly discovered that they had a close friend in common. They were shocked that they had not met sooner. Soon they were planning future opportunities to get together with the friend in common. The message is: look for connections in order to get to know people better.

Doing "Business" Together

The ideal common interest for a solopreneur is to connect about business. Finding people who have a need for what you can provide is the common interest that binds people in the free-enterprise economy. The economic process is the one by which the "customer" discovers they have a need and then discovers that the "entrepreneur" has the best solution. Many people become friends because they have done business together for a period of time. Today those friendships may be in person or online.

Connecting With Other Solopreneurs

There is great potential for all of us as solopreneurs to connect with each other, because of our unique business status. Soloists share many joys in common: landing an important piece of business, developing a marketing strategy that succeeds, solving a computer challenge, surviving an audit! Only another solopreneur can truly know what it is like to face a daunting challenge and prevail!

Ask Yourself:
How can I revitalize an existing relationship by using a common interest?

Think About It:
Solopreneurship is one of the common interests through which I can build a bridge to someone.

Remember:
Build on common ground to establish the connection for lasting relationships.

PART II

PROVIDE VALUE

...to Make a Difference

What people give to a relationship must be perceived as a reasonable exchange for what they get; this is the "marketing equation."

For relationships to survive and thrive, an exchange of value must exist. Sometimes what is given and what is received by each person is readily apparent. Regardless, people need to feel they are getting at least as much as they are giving. At times a person may be comfortable giving far more, but over time it should balance out.

Think about your key relationships with business associates, family, and friends.

For each relationship, reflect on three questions:

- What are you willing to give?
- What do you expect to get?
- Will it be mutually beneficial?

How you respond to these questions will reveal how you view the exchange of value. If you want to increase the value you provide, the next four chapters will help you do just that. They reveal how you can help other people, how you can provide value.

Know Your Niche

BEING IN THE RIGHT NICHE GIVES YOUR BUSINESS A SOLID FOUNDATION.

YOUR NICHE IS UNIQUE.

Being in the right niche is like wearing comfortable clothing and shoes...they fit you perfectly. If you wear shoes and clothes that fit, you feel, move, and look better. You can walk into a room and not even have to think about your clothing. As a result, you are free to concentrate on visiting with people.

However, if you wear clothes that are too big or small, you feel uncomfortable, embarrassed, and you lack confidence. Ill-fitting clothes leave you in search of an explanation or an excuse. When you walk into a room with clothes that don't fit, you want to hide! You have no desire to interact, no desire to connect!

When you are in a niche that fits your skills and experience, you face each day with confidence, optimism, and the belief that you can help others. This is exactly where you want to be when you begin relationships!

When you are in the right niche:
- You can serve others
- You can be authentic
- You can be dependable
- You can exceed expectations
- You can enjoy your business
- You have a great opportunity to build meaningful relationships
- You have your best chance to be successful

Understanding Niches
Niches, or niche markets, come in all sizes and

offer a great fit for solopreneurs. A niche market is a focused, targetable portion of a market. A business that focuses on a niche is addressing a need for a product or service that is not being addressed well by mainstream providers.

For example, instead of offering accounting services to businesses, a business could establish a niche market by specializing in accounting services for small businesses—which is what WorkingPoint.com has done.

Another example: Beth Buelow is a coach based in Washington state who serves solopreneurs — introverted solopreneurs!

Identify the Niche That Fits You
The ideal niche is one that:
1. You love.
2. You know very well…you're an expert.
3. Will buy what you're selling.
4. Is large enough for you and competitors.

Ask Yourself:

What subjects, topics, or activities could you work at, and discuss with authority, for hours and hours, and not get bored—and not be boring to others?

Think About It:

You have the potential within yourself to create new niches.

Remember:

A niche is an identifiable group of people for whom you would like to perform services.

If you pick a niche, you lose some customers.
If you don't pick a niche, you lose ALL customers.
— Naomi Dunford

We discover our role in life through our relationships with others.
— Rick Warren

Key #6

Serve Others

UNDERSTAND WHAT A PERSON
SEEKS AND THE VALUE YOU CAN
OFFER, THEN PROVIDE IT
AND MORE.

SERVING IS GIVING VALUE.

Serve others, everyone, as if they were your customers. As with any relationship, satisfaction and growth have everything to do with meeting expectations. Meeting expectations has to do with meeting people's needs. With an attitude of service, expectations are fulfilled, the relationship can gain significance, and it can last.

According to Ken Blanchard and Sheldon Bowles, a critical step in creating "raving fans" (the title of their book) as customers is to "discover what the customer wants."

To create raving fans in business and personal relationships, it's necessary to provide what they want and need. Here are insights about serving others:

- You have something unique to offer: your time, your energy, and your talent.
- What others value most may cost you very little time, effort, or money.
- Be willing to give before you expect to receive something back.
- Be willing to give more than you expect to get.
- Service involves attitudes and habits that apply to all relationships.
- Invest yourself in people; you will be rewarded.

Customers First—Relationships Forever

Regardless of your type of work, someone is a "customer" of what you do. If you're in business, it's a safe bet customers are your top priority. Ultimately, if you're focused on customers, the rest falls into place. That's why it's helpful to consider these questions:

- Who are my customers?
- What do my customers expect of me?
- How well am I doing, how can I do better?
- Why do my customers buy from me?
- Where should I focus to improve customer service?
- When will I do the new things that my customers need?

Ask Yourself:

What can I do to cultivate a servant's heart?

Think About It:

The simple act of paying attention can enhance my relationships.

Remember:

What I give to relationships is more important than what I get from them.

Serve Others

"How can I make people better as a result of connecting with me?…This is a strategy to connect with anyone, anywhere, any time."

— Jeffrey Gitomer

"The goal as a company is to have customer service that is not just the best, but legendary."

— Sam Walton

We have moved away from the era of the go-getter and we are now in the era of the "go-giver." Successful people are always looking for ways to do things for other people.

— Brian Tracy

Key #7

Go Beyond
Expectations

Going above and
beyond instills trust.

Be a "value-added" provider.

"Exceeding expectations" means going beyond standard performance for a situation. When you exceed expectations, you stand out from others. Going the extra mile helps establish integrity and build trust.

People who almost always meet and sometimes beat expectations can be counted on. They make good partners, friends, team members, and service providers. You can trust them, and that helps strengthen the connection. You want to have relationships with those people. And when you are trustworthy, others want to establish a relationship with you.

Build Loyalty

Meeting expectations might be fine when there is no competition. But exceeding expectations is the key to attracting and retaining customers in competitive situations. Think of your favorite restaurant, hair stylist, retailer, or suppliers for your business. They are the ones who do more than the others and usually more than you expect.

Under-promise and over-deliver in everything you do. For example, with deadlines, always build extra time into your schedule. This gives you a margin of error in case something goes wrong. If nothing goes wrong, the cushion allows you to deliver the product or service to the client earlier than expected.

Value-Added

The term "value-added" has been used to mean

a variety of things. We are using it to signify those things that you do to add value to your product or service and for which you do not charge the customer.

For example, Jim has a cleaning lady who comes to his apartment once a week (whether it needs it or not). She does all the normal cleaning of the apartment and does a wonderful job of ironing shirts and slacks…she would iron handkerchiefs if he did not get them in the drawer before she arrives. But the real value-added feature is the little note she writes to say, "Thank you, see you next week at 4:15 on Tuesday!" Jim does not usually see her, but he always sees her little note. It is a connection with a friend.

What do you do, or what could you do, that would be "value-added" for your niche of customers, products, and services?

Ask Yourself:

Whose expectations will I exceed today, tomorrow, and beyond?

Think About It:

Where would you rate if your business clients, family members, friends, and neighbors were to fill out a service questionnaire about you today? Below expectations? About average? Exceeds expectations?

Remember:

Exceeding expectations includes little things, not just big, dramatic, one-time events.

"There are no traffic jams along the extra mile."
— Roger Staubach

"Price is what you pay. Value is what you get."
— Warren Buffett

Do the Little Things

They add up!

Your greatest impact may come from the little things you do for others.

Making a difference in people's lives is not as difficult or costly as you might think. In fact, it's often the little things that make the greatest impact.

If you learn and practice a few basic inter-personal skills, it will enhance your relations-Doing the little things adds value to your prod-ucts and services—and to your friendships. The consistent use of your relationship-marketing skills helps other people feel important and appreciated. It will also help you reach a new level of value and respect in both new and existing relationships.

Interpersonal Skills that Provide Value

• **Smile.** Your smile warms the space around you and the people in it.

• **Respond promptly.** When you receive an e-mail, send a reply within 24 hours.

• **Remember and use names.** Everyone responds to the sound of their name. Don't you?

• **Be inquiring.** Ask questions that encourage people to talk about their favorite topics: me, myself, and mine (my family, my work, my success, my opinion).

• **Listen well.** Use all of your senses and your heart to listen intently.

• **Show genuine interest.** Your sincerity will be obvious.

Acts of Kindness for Everyday Life

In addition to the interpersonal skills, there are

small acts of kindness you can do for others. The publication of *Random Acts of Kindness* in 1993 sparked widespread interest in doing unexpected, but appreciated, acts of kindness for strangers. What if your acts of kindness weren't random and the recipients weren't strangers? Therein lies an opportunity for you to do little things for others, especially in relationships that are important to you.

You have the opportunity to serve people in all walks of life— family, friends, business associates, and passing acquaintances. Through your acts of kindness, the little things you do for others, you have the potential make a positive impact on someone's life. It may draw them closer, giving relationships a chance to grow.

The little things...

Add up…

Mean a lot…

Never go out of style...

Are readily available to give away…

Are always welcome…

Ask Yourself:
What is one thoughtful, unexpected thing I can do today to make a difference in someone else's life—at work, home or in a friendship?

Think About It:
If I give myself to others each day, I will never spend another day alone.

Remember:
Acts of kindness are small actions with big impact.

Focus on doing the right things in order to do things right.

— Leonard Finkel

I believe that small acts done with great love can change the world.

— Mother Teresa

PART III

ACT WITH INTEGRITY

Relationships thrive on a foundation of trust. Trust is having confidence in the integrity and loyalty of another person.

Trust between people is the bedrock of any relationship. Without it, a relationship has little chance of developing into something meaningful and lasting.

Rich, a financial planner with 40 years of experience handling sensitive client information, says you cannot move forward in a relationship until you establish trust.

This is true for every type of relationship.

Integrity and loyalty are essential to building trust. Integrity is honesty that you convey in word (by speaking the truth) and in deed (by doing what you say you will do).

Loyalty is a special kind of integrity that you express through your faithfulness to another person.

You probably can identify situations in your life when trust was gained because integrity and/or loyalty were present. Those are the types of relationships you should to seek to build.

Be Authentic

HAVE FAITH IN THE TRUE YOU.

REVEALING WHO YOU ARE FORMS THE BASIS FOR AUTHENTIC RELATIONSHIPS.

Webster's New Collegiate Dictionary defines authenticity as "…conforming to fact or reality; trustworthy; not imaginary, false, or imitation." Authenticity requires actions that are a true representation of yourself. The goal should be to act and speak in ways that are genuine.

Anything that hints of being fake, fraudulent, or phony lacks authenticity. If the basis for a relationship is distorted from the start, it may never progress. If it begins on a false note, it is likely to be destined for failure.

Our society values authenticity, but it takes courage, character, and confidence to show it. In the late 1960s, John Powell, S.J., wrote a book "Why am I afraid to tell you who I am?" His answer was, "I am afraid to tell you who I am, because, if I tell you who I am, you may not like who I am, and it's all that I have."

Distortion of Truth

We lack authenticity whenever we distort the truth about ourselves, intentional or not. Too often, in an attempt to paint the best possible picture, we try to impress, gain favor, or gain advantage.

Individuals and organizations distort the truth. You may not even realize you are doing it, or you may convince yourself that your intentions are good. Perhaps it is a habit.

Authentic Relationships

Authenticity reveals our character and creates trust, synergy, and connection with those around us. Bill George, former chairman and CEO of

Medtronic and author of *Authentic Leadership: Rediscovering the Secrets to Creating Lasting Value* believes authenticity is "being yourself; being the person you were created to be."

Marks of Authenticity

How do you know when you or someone else is being authentic? An indicator of authenticity is when people place the welfare of others first. Here are some examples:

• The authentic self discloses mistakes before mistakes are discovered by others, and does so even if the mistakes never would have been found.

• The authentic self is honest about his or her limitations. For example, if a new piece of business walks through your door but you do not have the expertise or the time to do the job, you are acting with authenticity by admitting your situation and referring the business to someone who is qualified to do the work.

Ask Yourself:
What are my real motives in a potential new relationship?

Think About It:
The more authentic you are, the more you respect yourself and others.

Remember:
A relationship without authenticity will fail.

We are authentic when we discern, seek, and live into truth, as persons in diverse communities and in the real world.
— Robert W. Terry

The real secret to gaining legitimacy is authenticity.
— Susan Baroncini-Moe

Earn and Give Trust

EARN TRUST AND GIVE TRUST TO OTHERS.

TRUST IS A SIGN OF CONFIDENCE IN THE FUTURE OF A RELATIONSHIP.

Trust is a requirement for any relationship. It is the foundation upon which to build strong, lasting relationships.

Relationships are based on the two-way communication between people, including written and spoken words, gestures, and actions. Your goal should be to act with integrity to assure that the information you provide to others is accurate.

That's because the truth about ourselves (including our ideas, beliefs, products, organizations) is at the core of a relationship built on trust. Anything that misleads others can lead to a lack of trust.

The reality is that quality relationships are built on principles—especially the principle of trust. And trust grows out of trustworthiness, out of the character to make and keep commitments, to share resources, to be caring and responsible, to belong, to love unconditionally.
— Stephen R. Covey

It Comes Down to... Telling the Truth

Truth is the glue that bonds people together. Trust is fertile ground in which other relationship qualities can germinate and grow, such as freedom to fail, risk-taking, empowerment, honesty, and openness. When you have trust among people, you increase the potential to achieve your goals in the relationship.

Trust is a two-way street. It needs to travel in

both directions: give your trust to another person by using words and actions that reveal your acceptance of them; gain the trust of another person by demonstrating trustworthiness through your integrity and loyalty. Both people have to give to gain trust.

Be First to Trust

With trust, it is important to lead. In some situations, you might need to take the risk of trusting others. Earning another person's trust may require that you be vulnerable and be the first one demonstrate that you trust. When you grant trust, the other person has the opportunity to prove their worthiness. This creates an opportunity for the relationship to develop.

You must learn to be a good judge of character and recognize when people can be trusted. Some people may want to be trustworthy, but for one reason or another they are unable to deliver on their promises. You have to be willing to walk away from relationships and deals that do not have this essential foundation of two-way trust.

Ask Yourself:
Am I willing to grant trust to others in my business, family, and social relationships?

Think About It:
Take the lead by granting a degree of trust to others.

Remember:
Trust is based on information about yourself.

To be trusted is a greater compliment than being loved.
— George MacDonald

The level of trust in business relationships— whether external or internal—is a greater determinant of success than anything else, including content excellence.
— Charles H. Green

Be Fair

INTEGRITY IS ALWAYS ON THE SIDE OF FAIRNESS.

FAIRNESS EARNS RESPECT.

We act with fairness toward others when we seek our business goals legitimately, when our pursuits are done properly and as promised and agreed. Fairness is often in the eyes of the beholder but here are some ways to be fair-minded.

Don't Take Advantage of a Customer's Lack of Knowledge

As a solopreneur, you often possess much more knowledge than your customers regarding your products or services. Typically this occurs early in a relationship.

When you are in an unequal power position with the client, it is vital that you place your client's needs above yours. You and your business might experience a temporary gain by taking advantage of your power position, but don't do it. In the long run, the relationship with your client will be much healthier.

Be Fair to Yourself on Pricing

It's easy to understand that you should be fair toward customers in pricing. It is just as important—and maybe more important—for you to be fair to yourself in pricing. Remember that you are doing more than providing a service—you are providing a solution. Never be afraid to charge for the value you provide. When you accept less than you are worth, you are planting seeds of resentment. If resentment grows, it will choke and kill the relationship.

Admit Mistakes

Fairness requires humility and honesty. In his book *Ten Positive Phrases For Positive People,*

Rich DeVos, cofounder of Amway and chairman of the Orlando Magic of the National Basketball Association, writes that saying "I'm wrong" is a powerful, positive act because it can: wash away the pain of a strained relationship, move a negotiation forward, end an argument, start a healing process, and even turn enemies into friends.

Make the Solution Better

After the printing of one of Jim's books, Jim discovered that the book's first page had the words "place cover here" in the middle of the page. Obviously, this was an enormous mistake, and it had the potential to be very expensive for the party who was at fault.

Jim knew that he and others could have and should have caught the mistake. Instead of trying to seek an advantage by blaming others, Jim acted with fairness: he told the printer that the focus should be on finding a solution, not on assigning blame. He said, "Let's see if we can find a solution that makes it better than it was ever intended."

Free to find a solution, the printer came up

with a brilliant one—an embossed sticker in the shape of the book's dominant image was created and used to cover the mistake. The resulting page is beautiful.

Ask Yourself:
In my pricing, am I being fair to myself and my family?

Think About It:
Go for what is right, not what can I get.

Remember:
The heartfelt admission of fault is an act of fairness—it's the "reset button" for relationships.

Individuals and organizations that can compete on generosity and fairness repeatedly defeat those that do it grudgingly.

— Seth Godin

Follow the Rules

RULES ARE PRESCRIBED GUIDELINES, EXPECTATIONS, OR BOUNDARIES FOR BEHAVIOR.

DO NOT CUT CORNERS.

Following the rules is a strong indicator of a person's integrity.

People you meet expect that you are following the rules. It's a reasonable expectation on their part, because rules are the basis for a civilized, functioning society. It's fashionable to talk about "not following the rules," but the truth is that without rules and laws—and people who abide by them—chaos results.

Rules for solopreneurs can take many forms. All of them are important, and here are a few examples:

Professional standards. Nearly every profession has codes of conduct that practitioners must follow if they are to remain in good standing in their professional community. Know and understand the standards for your profession and follow them meticulously.

Laws. It's likely that many local, state, and federal laws apply to your business. The laws can govern taxes, signage, building codes, safety, and much more. If you do not know the depth and breadth of these laws, hire an attorney who knows your business and industry, and have him or her evaluate your business.

Contracts essentially are rules that bind two parties. Prior to signing, always know and understand what your contract says. Even better, volunteer to have your attorney draft the contract—it ensures that you know what's in the fine print.

Industry customs. Every business has unwritten traditions and customs. If you've been in your business long enough, it's likely that you know the rules. If you are ever in doubt, ask a trusted colleague.

Breaking Rules Is Risky Business

The penalties for not following rules can be severe. If you don't play by the rules, don't expect sympathy, because you have broken the trust that individuals and a community have placed in you. Do you want an example of how rule-breaking can destroy people's lives? Here's one: Bernie Madoff. Enough said.

Not knowing the rules is not an adequate excuse, just as ignorance of the law is not a defense when you are caught going 65 miles per hour in a 55 zone. Not knowing can be just as bad as knowing and not following the rules.

Knowing and following the rules enhances trust within relationships and helps you sustain business success.

Ask Yourself:

Where have I been stretching the rules
too far?

Think About It:

What expectations or "rules" for my
behavior do I need to study (or ask about)
so that my integrity will be beyond question?

Remember:

There are rules to follow in every business
and social situation.

Breaking with the "same-old, same-old"
is a relationship-marketing strategy.
Breaking laws and disregarding ethical standards
is folly.

— Larry Keltto

PART IV

DEMONSTRATE RESPECT

...TO SHOW YOU CARE

**Positive words and deeds
demonstrate respect.**

Respect is another two-way street. It is important to show respect for others, and it's also important to gain respect from others. When you show respect for others, you demonstrate through your words and deeds that you accept and value them. To gain respect involves saying and doing things that show others you are worthy of their respect.

Respect is showing positive regard and believing every person has value. Without mutual respect, a relationship will not develop into something lasting and meaningful. The next four keys describe how to use relationship marketing to demonstrate respect and show that you care.

Take Care of Yourself

TO GIVE VALUE TO OTHERS, YOU MUST FIRST VALUE YOURSELF.

RECOGNIZE YOUR STRENGTHS.

When you are engrossed in business, it can take over your life. Solopreneurs need to maintain a balanced lifestyle. Balance means spending an appropriate amount of time at work, with family, and in recreation. This includes allowing appropriate time for the important people in our life.

The solopreneur life can be stressful. That is why it must include a healthy diet, recreation, social life, and just plain relaxing. When you find yourself out of balance or when others point this out to you, it is time to assess and make changes. When you care for yourself you're better prepared to care for others.

As a small business owner, you will need support. Emotional support, branding and design help, and having someone to bounce ideas off. I was lucky enough to find this in my best friend and business partner.

Jade Craven

Healthy "self-talk"

How you treat yourself has a profound effect on your attitudes, behavior, and success in your work and and your business relationships. A healthy respect for yourself helps you realize your potential.

In *Authentic Happiness,* the father of "positive psychology," Dr. Martin E. P. Seligman, writes that "Count your blessings" is one of the eight steps toward a more satisfying life. He developed "gratitude exercises" to help people count their blessings each day. An example is to list "three things about myself I value today." His research shows that reflecting on happiness makes people better, and it makes us more valued by others.

Our relationship with ourselves is revealed through our inner dialogue. Too often we send negative messages about ourselves, our work, or life in general. Since solopreneurs typically spend a lot of time working on their own, it is particularly important to have a positive self-image. This involves saying positive and encouraging things to yourself before, during, and after work.

Since you are influenced by what you tell yourself, the messages can set you up for defeat or help prepare you for success.

Repeated successes help you achieve your potential in business, sports, or other pursuits. Fortunately we are created with the capacity to value ourselves through self-awareness, positive feedback, and self-development.

Build on Strengths

People enjoy being with people who have a

positive and realistic sense of self-worth. These individuals tend to be efficient, accomplish more, and bring out the best in those around them.

In life and business it is important to recognize and utilize your uniqueness. It is probably your strengths that have allowed you to start your own business. Recognize what those strengths are and build upon them. Make sure your limitations do not undermine your success.

Use your strengths to help you connect with others. Your skills are likely to be capabilities that others admire about you. They are also likely to be skills that help you serve others. This helps you demonstrate respect to others. You do not have to attempt to duplicate some else's style or approach. You are unique and, therefore, you should have a style that reflects your physical, mental, and social attributes.

Ask Yourself:

How can I treat myself with more respect and admiration at work and in the rest of my life?

Think About It:

What do I discover when I pause to count my blessings in life?

Remember:

Utilize your strengths to your greatest advantage in your work.

Your chances of success in any undertaking can always be measured by your belief in yourself.
— Robert Collier

We need not only to encourage others, we need to encourage ourselves.
— Jim Sheard and Wally Armstrong

Take Care of Yourself

Care
For Others

CARING IS SHARING
SOME OF YOUR VALUE WITH
SOMEONE YOU VALUE.

CARING FULLY MEANS
WITHOUT RESTRAINT.

The prior key emphasized the importance of caring for yourself, so that you can care for others. When you feel good about yourself you have the capacity to give to others.

The theme of this key is to give concern, attention, and help to others. Your customers, family, friends, and even associates are people for whom you will want to demonstrate caring. Though you can't totally give yourself to everyone you meet, you can find ways to give care in relationships.

Treat others as you would like to be treated in the same situation.

Webster's definition of the verb "care" includes "to be concerned about and to give care." Synonyms include "pay attention, look after, keep an eye on, and keep watch." Our society admires those who care for others. Your business demands that you care for your customers; they will value your caring approach. Caring may be expressed as being:

- Attentive—detect the real need.
- Other-focused—put others before yourself.
- Creative—add new ways to serve.
- Satisfying—receiver feels benefited.

If you want to lift yourself up,
lift up someone else.

— Booker T. Washington

Increasing Your Value

In your business and in your personal life you can demonstrate respect by showing how much you care. To show you care:

1. Discover **what the person would value, appreciate, or need** at this moment. What does this person expect of you as their family member, friend, employee, or service provider? What would they most value in a time of need such as illness or sadness?

2. Identify **what you can give** that will be valued. You can only give out of what you have— interpersonal skills, time, and other resources.

3. Determine **what you are willing to do** to meet their expectations.

I look for long-term relationships with my clients, even though it's only a short-term project. I want to give them as much of my time as possible when we work together so I can nurture that relationship and show them that I really care about their business.

— Amy Harrison

It Really Shows

When you truly value others it shows in the things you say and do. It not only makes life more pleasant, but you demonstrate respect and show you care. Caring fully about someone is demonstrated by genuine interest, putting yourself in their shoes, wanting good things for them, and acting in their best interest.

You can also show respect by asking others for their opinion or advice, giving them your time and attention, dressing with respect for the person and situation, and offering to pay for something you share, like food, drinks, or an activity.

Some people are easier to respect than others, so as an exercise, take a moment to list family members, friends, peers, and clients/customers. Note the reasons why you respect each one.

Ask Yourself:
Do I care enough to give my very best to
my clients, family, friends, peers, and
companions?

Think About It:
What is your very best? What is it that you
have to give to your clients that is valued in
each of those relationships?

Remember:
Your clients will begin to care what you
know when they know that you care.

*Appreciating others gets you in the habit of
noticing more and more things to appreciate,
thus leading to an overall attitude of gratitude for
your life.*

— Susan Campbell

Care For Others

Dale Carnegie once wrote that the very best way to
build friendly relationships with others
is to become genuinely interested in them.
— Brian Tracy

Respect is one of the greatest gifts you can give to
another human being.
— Armida Russell

To have a friend you must be a friend.
— Rick Warren

Embrace Differences

DIFFERENCES AMONG PEOPLE CREATE OPPORTUNITIES.

INCLUDE A VARIETY OF PEOPLE.

Embrace differences by treating others with respect and dignity in all aspects of your life. This can be applied in your family, and business, and social settings.

We are inclined to think of difference in terms of gender, age/generations, race, national origin, religious beliefs, marital status, and abilities. But other differences are socioeconomic level, occupation, personality, style, point of view, and educational background.

Accept and seek diversity. It is the right thing to do and, ultimately, it strengthens your business.

Attitude of Inclusiveness

Embrace means to include, receive, welcome, and cherish. To embrace differences is more than simply accepting. It is being active and inclusive. To embrace differences is to actively welcome and participate with people who are different from you. You may embrace differences in order to benefit someone else, but do not overlook the benefit to yourself.

Thrivers work in harmony with others—
they respect and honor differences.
— David McNally

Diversity in Business

Recognizing differences and exploring possibilities can build your business. Here are a few examples we have come across:

1. A **lawncare professional** recognized that

many elderly people could not handle the tasks involved and he reached out to help them, even though it was a different group from his existing business clients.

2. A **local sub sandwich shop** discovered the need for a "very rapid" delivery service for people having lunch at home or work.

3. A group of women in Northfield, Minnesota, decided to call themselves **"The Dirty Ladies."** They plant flower gardens for people who no longer have the ability.

Ask Yourself:
Do I have an opportunity to embrace differences today?

Think About It:
A slight tweaking might make your business very attractive to a group of people you are not currently serving.

Remember:
The embracing of differences creates opportunities to make an impact.

You can do what I cannot do.
I can do what you cannot do.
Together we can do great things.
— Mother Teresa

Be A Team Player

IN MEETING THEIR NEEDS, THINK OF YOUR CUSTOMERS AS TEAMMATES.

YOUR FAMILY AND FRIENDS ARE PART OF YOUR TEAM; GIVE THEM YOUR BEST EFFORT.

Teamwork Works

In business we recognize that it is impossible to do everything ourselves. Even as solopreneurs we must rely on others to provide us with services we are not capable of performing. It may be a printer, Internet provider, graphic designer, editor, or computer repair service. We think of ourselves as being "solo," but in reality we are a team.

Determining whom to add to the team is an important function of the solopreneur. Recognizing and valuing these different skills will help you achieve your own goals. Sometimes these associates may also rely on your strengths and services to help them achieve their goals.

Utilizing everyone's strengths helps a team. All can contribute, feel valued, maximize strengths, and minimize limitations. This is often true when you are working with a client. They bring experience and you bring your talent and expertise. Working together, you can provide the customer with solutions—not just services.

What gives a team richness, texture, and, ultimately, resourcefulness is the uniqueness of its members and an artful linking of their diverse gifts.

— Allan Cox

Teaming with Other Professionals

One opportunity that exists for many solopreneurs is to team with others in providing a service or product.

This book is an example. It is the combined effort of two solopreneurs who were acquaintances before they discovered their common interest in writing a book like this. Larry has many years of experience coaching solopreneurs and in writing. He has an excellent Web site for gathering and distributing information that is helpful to his clients. Jim had written a book on relationships, with golfers as the primary audience, but the principles of relationship-building were equally applicable to entrepreneurs. Thus, Larry and Jim became a team.

You may have already teamed with other professionals to provide services and products to individuals or businesses. It requires cooperation and the need to share in decisions and workload. Teaming with others allows you to do things that could not otherwise be accomplished. For example, the challenge of completing this book would have been too great if it were not for the combined skills and background of both Larry and Jim.

**All people have a style
that is the reflection of their experiences,
talents, beliefs, habits, and mindset.**

**Just because you spend time working
on your own does not mean you are not a
member of a team.**

Serving on Teams

Another way of experiencing teamwork is to participate on teams that serve the community or your profession. This can occur by serving on committees and boards. It can also be a part of participating in professional associations that fit you line of work. Becoming active in these opportunities is a way of meeting people, perhaps identifying prospects, building your own skills, and helping others.

But being overly active in these outside activities is not recommended, as it can take away too much time from your business and family. The right opportunities, when well-timed, can provide great satisfaction and growth.

Ask Yourself:

Am I missing opportunities to form a team with other solopreneurs to provide outstanding service to selected clients?

Think About It:

Have you been on a team where people with diverse skills and backgrounds made a significant contribution or achieved a challenging goal together? What did you learn?

Remember:

You and your client are a team that is well-designed to meet the client's needs.

Be A Team Player

I worked to form coalitions with fellow business owners, create a referral train, and donate my services in little ways when I could.

— Laura Petrolino

Get a good network. I not only have a great network of clients and partners locally, I am also active in the Third Tribe forums, and the advice is invaluable.

— Heather Claus

PART V

COMMUNICATE WITH PURPOSE

…to Strengthen Understanding

Connect with people with common interests to create opportunities for relationships to emerge.

It may be a chance encounter, such as meeting a new member of your service organization, or it can be an intentional meeting with a prospective client. These are called "connections." They are the initial step in building a relationship.

To proactively seek connections, it helps to ask these three questions:

• What are my goals in my business and in life?

• How can relationships help me achieve those goals?

• Who do I want to meet to continue to achieve those goals?

The truth is, you don't always know how a relationship will benefit you or the other person. The key is to connect in a way that gives the relationship an opportunity to grow and thrive.

Key #17

Ask Questions

QUESTIONS HELP YOU
CONVERSE WITH PURPOSE.

PEOPLE LOVE TO TELL OTHERS
ABOUT THEMSELVES.

Conversations are the primary way we communicate in relationships. Conversations are comprised of questions, answers, comments, body language, and gestures. They may be face-to-face, on the phone, in e-mail, or online.

Conversations often are formalized into patterns we call interviews, meetings, sales calls, and counseling. One or more of these may be particularly important in your solo business venture and each of them is a set of skills in itself.

The Internet and social media create a different kind of conversation, those in which we are not face-to-face. This creates special demands since we do not have the benefit of seeing the reactions and tone of the other person, nor do they see ours.

Converse With Purpose

The mental preparation for a conversation included determining your purpose, preparing your questions, and anticipating various talking points related to your topic and purpose. The purpose of any conversation usually falls into one or more of these categories:

1. Have fun. Pass the time. Enjoy each other.

2. Build connection. Get acquainted. Be a friend.

3. Provide encouragement. Support. Offer advice.

4. Exchange information. Share topics of common interest.

5. Convince others. Persuade to your point of view, your product, your service

We seldom specify the purpose of each conversation, but at times it is fruitful. By clarifying the purpose, in your own mind, and perhaps with the other person, you can be more focused. You can ask good questions, listen, and encourage. Ideally there is a comfortable ebb and flow across topics and purposes. While not everything discussed will relate directly to a specific purpose, at the end it is good to know the purpose was met.

Questions With Purpose

Generally speaking, the best questions show interest and encourage the other person to provide information related to the purpose for the conversation. In *The Seven Powers of Questions: Secrets to Successful Communication in Life and at Work,* Dorothy Leeds describes seven ways questions are a powerful communication tool. They may be used to:

1. Demand or encourage **answers**
2. Stimulate **thinking**
3. Give valuable **information**
4. Put you in **control** or help people achieve purposes

5. Get people to **open up**
6. Inspire quality **listening**
7. Get people **persuaded**

While some of these purposes can be manipulative, questions can be used positively to show interest and caring, and to gather information for conversation and contribution. Questions are more likely to be seen as positive, and focused on the purpose of the conversation, when they are:

1. **Open-ended;** cannot be answered with one word; encourage talking.
2. **Contribute** to the topic and purpose(s) for the conversation and relationship.
3. **Thought-provoking;** invite meaningful, insightful contributions.
4. **Well-timed;** fit the context of the conversation.
5. **Positive and polite,** asked in a manner that is open to the response.
6. **Show effective listening** to what has been said; explore what was said.

7. **Balance** the opportunity for contributions from all those involved.

Examples of open-ended questions are:

1. What is your biggest business challenge right now?
2. What is your favorite computer business program; and why?
3. How is your new marketing approach working?
4. What are your goals for the next six months and three years ?

Topics can be explored with open-ended questions like:

How's it going? How's your _____ ?

Tell me about your _____ ?

Earlier you mentioned _____ . Tell me more about that.

Comments made in a conversation can be followed up with open-ended inquiries (or statements implying a question) such as:

"Tell me more."

"That's interesting." …with a pause that suggests you'd like to hear more.

"Why?" or ""Why is that? (asked politely to show interest).

"How (When, Where) did that happen?"

Ask Yourself:

What is my purpose for meeting (in person, on phone, online) with this person?

Think About It:

What questions can I ask that will improve the quality of our conversation and help me connect with this person?

Remember:

When you converse with purpose you develop relationships and have your needs met.

Listen Up!

LISTENING SHOWS INTEREST.

LISTEN WITH OPEN EARS, EYES, MIND, AND HEART.

Every conversation is an exchange of information. Questions are one of the keys to this exchange; listening is another. Questions open the window to the person with whom you are conversing. Listening is the way we hear what is going on inside. In combination they provide opportunity to get to know clients and customers.

Make a Difference

When you listen to learn, you develop opportunities to influence people and impact results. Why? People value those who listen to them.

The most successful solopreneurs are those who listen, because they seem polite, interested, and caring. We like them because they make us feel important and connected.

Most people want to make a positive impact in the lives of those around them. We want our lives to count for something. We want to be appreciated and valued. Listening is one of the surest ways to satisfy this need. Listening strengthens trust and deepens our commitment to a relationship.

Listening is one of the best ways to show respect.

Feeling valued is a powerful motivator. Influential people understand this. They listen to people. If you listen, you will learn things that can help you achieve your business goals. People have ideas that are valuable, but they need to be given an outlet to share them.

Learn to Listen; Listen to Learn

Listening is an important way to learn about people. What we learn is useful in serving others and meeting our own needs. By listening we can discover the answers to our questions, insights about others, concerns they may be feeling, and opportunities to help them.

With listening you gather information about:

1. **The person**—their opinions, concerns, interests, attitudes, feelings.
2. **Their knowledge or information** about an area of common interest.
3. **Their reactions** to you or what you offer them.

Authentic listening is not easy. It requires concentration. With attentive listening, you learn and you have the opportunity to build relationships.

Opportunity in Listening

Active listening doesn't come naturally to most people, but listening is worth the effort because when you listen, you have the opportunity to:

1. **Strengthen** relationships
2. Generate **trust** between people
3. Build **commitment** for new ways of doing business

4. Generate **ideas** that have lasting impact

It is important to initiate situations where you have an opportunity to listen to the other person. Depending upon the purpose, stage of the relationship, and interests of those involved, you can find opportunities to listen and to be heard.

In most business situations there is the need to sell your service or products. This involves telling prospects what you offer. But it is more important to listen for what it is wanted or needed. Only then can you show how your offer will fulfill the need.

Seek Opportunity… To Listen
- Be available
- Recognize opportunities
- Create opportunities

Hear Opportunity… When You Listen
- Focus on the person
- Have an open mind
- Discover concerns; seek insights about them

Act on Opportunity… After You Listen

• Get more information as needed
• Decide what action to take
• Take action!

Focus to LISTEN

Look at the person as you listen.
Inquire to show interest and clarity.
Seek to understand. Be sincere.
Talk to ask questions. Give feedback.
Encourage people to talk.
No judging is having an open mind.

**People want to know you heard
what they said.
They want to know
that you understood how they felt.**

Ask Yourself:
Does my listening demonstrate an attitude of "Tell me more!"?

Think About It:
People with influence learn to listen and listen to learn.

Remember:
You have a greater effect on others by the way you "listen" to them than by the way to "talk" to them.

The greatest gift you can give another
is the purity of your attention.
— Richard Moss

It is hard to listen when you are talking. Watch,
listen, and learn. You can't know it all yourself.
— Donald Trump

KEY #19

Encourage Others

BEING APPRECIATED IS A
UNIVERSAL DESIRE.

SINCERE COMPLIMENTS COST
NOTHING AND EARN DIVIDENDS.

Martin Seligman, the father of positive psychology, says "interpersonal virtues" such as helping others are important for our own well being and for serving others. "Invest time and energy in friends and family" is one of his "Eight Steps Toward a More Satisfying Life." (in the book *Authentic Happiness*).

Encouraging one another is something friends do. Tony Dungy, former head coach of the Indianapolis Colts of the National Football League, wrote in his book *Quiet Strength*: "God gives each one of us unique gifts, abilities, and passions."

How well we use those qualities to have an impact on the world around us determines how 'successful' we really are."

What Is Encouragement?

To encourage means to provide words, actions, or support that help people believe in themselves or take positive action.

On the next page is a list of needs and the ways people can be helped with encouragement.

The list looks like a job description of any coach. It is also a description of what many solo-preneurs do as part of their work. It is not always their primary job, but it is one of the important elements of serving people. Of course, parents, teachers, trainers, and friends act as coaches too.

Person's Need	How To Encourage
Feedback	Give specific examples and observations
Confidence	Give praise
Encouragement	Offer positive reinforcement, replace negatives
Support	Be available to listen, discuss, and help
Decisions	Help identify options, review pros and cons
Information	Provide information, places, or resources
Skills	Observe, give feedback, find resources
Insights/Wisdom	Share experiences, help find source
Inspiration	Help see possibilities, be a sounding board
Nurture	Express care, keep in touch
Acceptance	Be available, provide attention

Everyone has opportunities to encourage others as a team member, coworker, friend, spouse, or family member. The key in all these roles is to identify who needs encouragement, what will be most helpful, and how to provide the support. It requires the right skills and a willingness to apply those skills appropriately.

Why Encourage?

Encouraging others takes effort. There are benefits and costs, but it:

1. Is simply the right thing to do.
2. Helps build relationships.
3. Gives you influence in career, home, and community.
4. Helps teammates and, therefore, may improve your team performance.
5. Is a positive personality characteristic.

Being an encourager may cost you time, be inconvenient, and distract from other priorities. But the benefits will almost always outweigh the costs.

Become an Encourager

Some people are naturally gifted encouragers. Watch and learn from them. If encouraging others doesn't come naturally to you, take the suggestions below to heart. These are skills you can learn, they will begin to feel more natural. Remember that it is important to stay true to your personality and style. Don't try to be someone you're not. In your own style and in your own words and gestures, encourage someone today.

Encouraging requires being willing to:

1. **Slow down.** Step back and be available.
2. **Notice.** Be aware of others' needs and listen.
3. **Focus on others.** Develop compassion.
4. **See priorities differently.** Place people above tasks.
5. **Be willing to stop.** Pause what you are doing.
6. **Be willing to risk** getting involved or being rejected.
7. **Have tools for encouragement.** Keep a supply of note cards, send e-mail.

What can you say, ask, or do to encourage someone today?

Ask Yourself:
Do I live by the motto, "Be liberal with praise"?

Think About It:
Helping other people will always give you a boost, too.

Remember:
Observe positive things in people and let them know the positives you see.

If you train your mind to search for the positive things about other people, you will be surprised at how many good things you can observe in them and comment upon.

— Alan Loy McGinnis

*Too often we underestimate the power of a touch,
a smile, a kind word, a listening ear, an honest
compliment, or the smallest act of caring,
all of which have the potential to turn a life
around.*

— Leo Buscaglia

*Write and send one unnecessary note to someone
every day.*

— Jim Dimick

ENCOURAGE OTHERS

Seek Feedback

Feedback helps you keep on track.

Feedback helps us answer the question, "How can I do better?"

One big challenge of being a solopreneur is that you do not have the built-in feedback that exists in a typical business structure, with a supervisor, peers, and people you serve. All of them are sources of feedback. Many organizations have performance-management tools, peer feedback questionnaires, and customer surveys to provide individuals and teams with information to help evaluate and improve performance.

The solopreneur is, by definition, working alone in his or her business. There is nobody above, below, or at the same level to provide feedback. But if you look and listen, and seek it, you can acquire feedback. The sources are customers, peers in related businesses, and coaches who specialize in giving feedback to solopreneurs.

Ask For Feedback

Seek feedback by asking questions about your performance. It is important to assure the evaluator that you really do want their honest feedback. Tell them it will be helpful to you in serving others.

One way to obtain feedback is in writing. People often are reluctant to take the time to give feedback, but two or three well-stated questions like the ones below are not too much to ask a client after you have completed a project or series of projects for them:

• How am I doing?

• How can I do better?

• Based on my work, would you be inclined to refer me to your colleagues?

Questionnaire For Feedback

Heidi Koopman is a freelance graphic designer in Minneapolis. She calls her business Purpose Design. She did an outstanding job designing the cover and inside design for a book Jim co-authored with Lenore Else, *Fingerprints of Faith: Evidence of Things Not Seen.* People who see the book invariably comment on the beautiful green cover that features an embossed fingerprint over-laying an enlarged leaf. The theme and color is carried to the pages inside.

After the project was completed, Heidi sent a questionnaire that she had obtained from the Evangelical Free Church in America, seeking feedback about her work and the working rela-tionship in the project. Having such a question-naire demonstrated Heidi's professionalism and her commitment to the relationship.

Even though many of us have grown weary of filling out questionnaires, an approach like Heidi's is something nearly everyone will be will-ing to complete. Send the questionnaire right after the work has been completed, keep it short and easy to complete, and ask the person in advance if they would be willing to help you by providing feedback in a questionnaire.

Coaches as a Source of Feedback

It is particularly important for solopreneurs to seek feedback about their businesses. Coaches who specialize in working with solopreneurs can often focus on their unique needs.

Questions from coaches often are a version of the following:

1. How can you solve this problem?

2. How can you meet this new opportunity?

People who help with these issues may be professional coaches and mentors. Friends or peers who have faced the same issues can be helpful, too.

Ask Yourself:
Who would be knowledgeable and willing to give me feedback on how well I have been doing my work?

Think About It:
Feedback is your greatest source of ideas for improvement.

Remember:
You cannot coach yourself.

Yearn to understand first and to be understood second.

— Beca Lewis Allen

SEEK FEEDBACK

PART VI

SHARE
EXPERIENCES

...to Achieve Goals

**Shared experiences are opportunities to
interact with another person in a common
task or activity. They nourish and sustain
relationships.**

Through shared experiences, you have the opportunity to solidify connections in family, business, or social relationships.

You can strive to be friendly, considerate, and service-oriented in your day-to-day activities. Beyond that, you can:

• Identify the important people in your life.

• Intentionally plan shared experiences with them, and use your interpersonal skills to build stronger and more lasting connections.

By creating shared experiences that are enjoyable and valuable to others, you demonstrate your commitment to them and influence their commitment to you in return. Shared experiences that bond people may be once-in-a-lifetime events, but typically they are the accumulation of small moments of life experienced together.

KEY #21

Build
On Interests

BUSINESS OPPORTUNITY
BRINGS PEOPLE TOGETHER.

SEEK OPPORTUNITIES
TO ENHANCE YOUR
MOST IMPORTANT
RELATIONSHIPS.

Once a connection with another person begins, you must do your part to keep it going. Shared experiences are the things you do with your contacts that build upon the foundation of common interests. They create new, lasting memories and provide opportunities to give and receive value. It takes effort and a thoughtful strategy.

An "opportunity" is a relationship-building

experience that:
- **Fits** with your goals for the relationship.
- **Enhances** the relationship.
- **Builds** connection, depth, and commitment.
- **Provides** value to the other person.

Building connections involves shared experiences that make the connection stronger, more meaningful, longer lasting, and more resilient. People who achieve lofty goals set a course for building connections.

Think About and Plan…
- **Who** should I target for building a better relationship?
- **What** do I want to accomplish in the relationship?
- **How** can I make it happen?

1. Who?
Everyone has relationships they want to build. Determine which ones you want to prioritize. Take notes on details such as the date, the points

of conversation, and follow-up tasks. For the solopreneur this includes your clients and prospective clients.

2. What To Do With Them? When and Where?

Opportunities to build relationships may be short or long, spontaneous or planned, inexpensive or expensive. Small opportunities for building connections include phone calls, greeting cards, e-mails, meeting for coffee, lunch, or doing a favor.

Big opportunities take more time, money, or preparation. They could include celebrations, dining, or attending a play. It is not the size or expense of the event but the shared experience that is most important.

3. How To Execute My Plan?

Shared opportunities require taking the initiative and identifying common interests. Your focused attention on the individuals with whom you want to build the relationship becomes a priority. Executing your plan also involves using the skills of serving others, knowing your role, and doing the little things.

Shared Vision

Shared vision grows out of shared interests. Wes Cantrell and James R. Lucas, authors of *High Performance Ethics,* make a statement that applies to many important personal relationships. "HPE (high performance ethics) leaders think about building on intangible ground—shared vision, mission, values, strategies—rather than thinking of the tangible elements they can see and understand."

Shared vision is possible and important for the longest lasting and most meaningful friendships, business partnerships, and marriages.

For example, the decision to marry is best based on a shared vision of what it will be like to be partners in life, "for life."

Or a copywriter speaks of her relationship with her largest client in a way that relates their shared vision of what the communications will be for the client's organization. According to Cantrell and Lucas, with a shared vision it is possible to develop an "integration plan" to determine how to merge common and differing interests. Since there will surely be differences (in interests, values, availability, etc.) there is the need to "face differences" and "share responsibility."

Ask Yourself:

What can I do to create a "shared vision" of with my clients?

Think About It:

Who? What? and How? … key questions to seek opportunities to build relationships.

Remember:

Your primary shared interest is your client's success and your client's satisfaction with your service.

Build On Interests

So rule number one for deepening your friendships is: Assign top priority to your relationships.
— Alan Loy McGinnis

KEY #22

Enjoy the Process

THINK POSITIVE THOUGHTS;
BRIGHTEN YOUR DAY.

LEARN FROM THE PAST;
PLAN FOR THE FUTURE;
LIVE IN THE MOMENT.

"Live in the moment." The idea is to not worry about what is behind you, nor about what is ahead of you, but to enjoy what is going on in your life in the present.

Certainly you as a solopreneur can learn from the past and make plans for the future, but enjoying the process is critical.

"Appreciative Inquiry"

Being appreciative is a wonderful quality. In fact, "appreciative inquiry" is a field of study in organization development.

As conceived by Dr. David Cooperrider, the term is derived from combining "appreciate" and "inquire" as they apply to organization, team, and individual performance. He uses these definitions:

"Appreciate"—1. recognize the best in people or the world around us; affirm past and present strengths, successes, and potentials; 2. increase in value. Synonyms: valuing, esteeming, and honoring.

"Inquire"—1. explore and discover; 2. ask questions; be open to seeing new potentials and possibilities. Synonyms: discovery, systematic exploration, study.

James Gregory Lord wrote, "Appreciative inquiry is...about heightening our awareness of the value, strength, and potential of ourselves and others—and overcoming the limits that we impose, often unconsciously, on our own capabilities." "By asking positive questions, we can generate new images of the future…images evoked by the best of the past and present."

Positive Activities

Here are some types of activities that are both positive and inquiring. They will help you look at your life in a positive light, ask good questions, and be nicer to yourself.

1. Read something positive each day. It may be a devotional or inspirational book.

2. Participate in a conference or clinic on a topic that would help you grow.

3. Have lunch once a week with an encouraging friend.

4. Take time to pause and eat a good meal—morning, noon, and evening.

5. Include exercise in your daily schedule.

6. Make a list of your most positive qualities and put it on your computer table.

Positive Questions

Inquire into the big picture:

1. What is the best part of my business venture?
2. What am I doing properly?
3. What are my strengths?
4. How can I continue to develop each of those strengths?

Review my day:

5. What did I do best today?
6. What positive things can I take away from my experience today?
7. What did I enjoy most about the people in my life today?

React to an activity:

8. What did I learn from the activity I just completed?
9. How is that an improvement over times in the past?

Review your strategy:

10. What is best/wisest part of the strategy for my business?

Ask Yourself:
When do I tend to be negative about life?

Think About It:
Are there parts of your life or work where
you would benefit from appreciative inquiry?

Remember:
One of the main reasons you became a
solopreneur was so you would be happy in
your daily work.

*Learning how to slow down and enjoy the present
is a wonderful gift to yourself and will help you
produce really high-quality work.*
— Pamela Slim

*You are indeed carrying within yourself
the potential to visualize, to design, and to create
an utterly satisfying, joyful, and pure lifestyle.*
— Rainer Maria Rilke

Enjoy the Process

Celebrate Success and Life!

CELEBRATE, CELEBRATE, CELEBRATE!

CELEBRATION IS THE COMMEMORATION OF A RELATIONSHIP EXPERIENCE.

To celebrate is to have a ceremony or festivity that marks a special occasion or event. It is usually joyous and shared with someone else. When we think of a celebration we tend to think of the big events: holidays, awards celebrations, graduations, and charity dinners. The best celebrations are the ones that celebrate small gains, new relationships, and business successes. Sharing a favorite memory with those who participated with you is like celebrating all over again.

Consciously celebrating even small accomplishments and occasions is a day brightener. The experience does not have to big or planned. It may be as simple as a coffee break, lunch, a spoken "thank you," or a small gift. Celebrations of all sizes add joy and create memories by calling attention to something good. If you take advantage of opportunities to celebrate, you will have more fun and be more fun to be around.

Rituals of Celebration

There are rituals of celebration in all shared relationship experiences. Watch groups of people when they meet for lunch. They enjoy a ritual of greeting, discussion, ordering, eating, and departure. They may shake hands or hug when they meet, and again when they depart. They may schedule the next meeting.

Most solopreneurs would benefit from more

celebration in their lives. Here are thoughts about how to do it.

What to Celebrate
- Accomplishments/achievements— your own and other people's
- Progress and milestones along the way; targets like…"We're halfway there."
- Opportunities you earn, or that just occur
- Time and special occasions with friends and family
- Life itself; the joy of life
- Momentary successes
- Being part of something bigger…teams, volunteers, family

How to Create More Celebration…
- A positive attitude; it helps you see joy along the way
- Seek different things to celebrate; be creative
- Be inclusive; include others; help others celebrate

- Be expansive; broaden ways you celebrate;
- Add surprise and spontaneity—a "surprise" party, note, dinner, coffee
- Identify little things to celebrate in family and your business
- Celebrate the "small positives;" it does not have to be a huge happening
- Reinforce good, better, best behavior; improvement; yours and others'
- Make memories in relationships by celebrating
- Do not miss opportunities

Celebration is about people, memories, togetherness, and keeping our eyes on goals. At other times it is nice to make family members or friends feel special with days of celebration.

There are so many ways to say "You are special!" even if it is not their birthday or anniversary.

Let people know they are special to you. Celebrate your own life. Enjoy yourself, utilize your talent, and encourage people.

Ask Yourself:
When was the last time I celebrated one of
my accomplishments?

Think About It:
Someone in my life deserves a
congratulatory call or note right now.

Remember:
A celebration is the punctuation mark
following a "shared experience" that makes a
statement about your life.

Business is Great!
People are Wonderful!
Life is Terrific!

— Giant Freeway Billboard for
Rob Gregory's Rochester Ford,
Rochester, Minnesota

Celebrate Success and Life!

These are the golden years,
therefore the golden days,
therefore the golden moments.
— Henry David Thoreau

The joy of life is made up of seemingly mundane
victories that give us our own small satisfactions.
— Billy Joel

Follow-Through

THE FIRST GOAL OF FOLLOW-THROUGH IS TO STAY CONNECTED.

FOLLOW-THROUGH BUILDS UNDERSTANDING AND CORRECT MISUNDERSTANDING.

Follow-through means doing what you said you would do for the relationship. Follow-through helps prevent, identify, and/or mend problems that would otherwise damage a relationship. It also creates opportunities to strengthen your relationships. If you tell your client, children, spouse, business partner, or friend that you will do something, get it done.

A high-level executive played in a pro-am golf event with Wayne Gretzky. Widely acclaimed as the greatest hockey player ever, Gretzky distinguished himself from other celebrity golfers by showing sincere interest in the amateurs. Starting at the first tee and throughout the round, he demonstrated humility and treated others equally. At the banquet, Gretzky asked questions, remembered names, and brought up details discussed during the round. Without being asked, he promised to send hockey mementos to the hockey-loving son of one of the amateurs, and Gretzky actually sent the items. By outgiving what was expected, Gretzky showed he was a man who strives to keep his promises.

Types of Follow-Through

- **Do what you said;** deliver on your promise or commitment.
- **Do your best;** follow up to check on it.
- **Stay connected**…despite time and distance.
- **Be there when needed,** expected or not.

- **Check back;** avoid surprises.
- **Adapt to needs,** change as needed.
- **Correct what is wrong;** take action.
- **Forgive;** be willing to move forward.
- **Be humble;** it can help heal a wound and mend a relationship.

Even when we do our best, we make mistakes. Those mistakes may cost us the relationship, or create irreparable lack of trust. Once the mistake has been made, the most important action will be the next one you make. Perhaps you can follow-through and recover the relationship. If not, at least you can learn to not make the mistake again.

Follow-through means fulfilling your commitment to seek success.

Ask Yourself:
Am I putting myself in a position to finish strongly with good follow-through in my most important relationships?

Think About It:
A short, nicely written thank-you note is rarely forgotten.

Remember:
When relationships fall apart or drift away, it's usually because the purpose is no longer there or someone did not follow through.

Coming together is a beginning; keeping together is progress; working together is success.
— Henry Ford

Bibliography

Allen, Beca Lewis, in David Mcnally, *The Eagle's Secret: Success Strategies for Thriving at Work & In Life,* Delacorte Press, New York, 1998, p. 177, ISBN 0-385-31427-2.

Baroncini-Moe, Susan, CEO of Business in Blue Jeans, in *www.lifehack.org/articles/management/are-you-authentic-in-your-small-business.html.*

Bolton, Robert, People Skills: *How to Assert Yourself, Listen to Others, and Resolve Conflicts,* A Touchstone Book, Simon & Schuster, New York, 1979, p. 78, ISBN 0-671-62248-X Pbk.

Brooks, Mark, In Lehman, Tom with Wubbels, Lance, *A Passion for the Game,* Bronze Bow Publishing, Minneapolis, Minnesota, 2005, p. 100, ISBN 1-932458-35-2.

Bryan, William Jennings, in David McNally, *The Eagle's Secret,* p. 143

Campbell, Susan, *Saying What's Real: 7 Keys to Authentic Communication and Relationship Success,* An H J Kramer Book, Tiburon, California, 2005, p. xxi., 85, ISBN 1-932073-12-4.

Cantrell, Wes and Lucas, James R., *High Performance Ethics: 10 Timeless Principles for Next-Generation Leadership,* Tyndale House Publishing, Inc., Carol Stream, Illinois, 2007, p. 127, 136, 137, 156.

Cashman Kevin, *Leadership from the Inside Out.*

Claus, Heather, 365 Days of Everything, www.365daysofeverything.com, Wilmington, North Carolina.

Collier, Robert, in Leonard Finkel, *The Secrets to the Game of Golf and Life,* Successful Library, Successories, 1997, ISBN 1-880461-41-42.

Cooperrider, David L. and Whitney, Diana, "A Positive Revolution in Change: Appreciative Inquiry"Appreciative Inquiry Commons, http://appreciativeinquiry.case.edu/intro/whatisai.cfm.

Covey, Steven R., *First Things First: To Live, to Love, to Learn, to Leave a Legacy,* Simon & Schuster, New York, 1994, p. 27, 57, ISBN: 0-671-86441-6.

Craven, Jade, Social Media Solutions, www.JadeCraven.com,

Bibliography

Geelong, Victoria, Australia.

DeAngelis, Barbara, *Real Moments: Discover the Secret for True Happiness,* New York, 1994, ISBN 0-440-50729-4.

DeVos, Rich, cofounder of Amway and chairman of the Orlando Magic of the National Basketball Association, *Ten Positive Phrases For Positive People.*

D'Onofrio, Vincent, brainyquote.com.

Drucker, Peter, brainyquote.com.

Duc de La Rochefoucauld, Francois, French author (1613-1680), in Richard Shea (editor), *The Book of Success,* Rutledge Hill Press, Nashville, Tennessee, 1993, p.114, ISBN 1-55853-254-4.

Dunford, Naomi, Ittybiz.com.

Dungy, Tony, *Quiet Strength,* p. 143.

Ellison, Larry, Thinkexist.com.

Finkel, Leonard, in *The Secrets to the Game of Golf and Life.*

Ford, Henry, in Ken Melrose, *Making the Grass Greener on Your Side,* p. 53.

George, Bill, *Authentic Leadership: Rediscovering the Secrets to Creating Lasting Value,* Jossey-Boss, San Francisco, California, 2003, ISBN 0-7879-6913-3.

Gitomer, Jeffrey, Jeffrey Gitomer's *Little Black Book of Connections: 6.5 ASSETS for Networking Your Way to RICH Relationships,* Bard Press, Austin, TX, ISBN 1-885167-66-0, 978-1-885167-66-8.

Godin, Seth, marketing guru, SethGodin.com

Green, Charles H., Trusted Advisor Associates, trustedadvisor.com/cgreen.articles/38/Trust-in-Business-The-Core-Concepts.

Harrison, Amy, Harrisonamy Copywriting, www.harrisonamy.com, Brighton, England.

Joel, Billy, in David McNally, *The Eagle's Secret: Success Strategies for Thriving at Work & In Life,* Delacorte Press, New York, 1998, p. 143, ISBN 0-385-31427-2.

Lake, Tony, *Relationships: The Complete Guide to Understanding Yourself and Other People,* Michael Joseph Limited, London, 1981, p. 58.

Leeds, Dorothy, *The Seven Powers of Questions: Secrets to*

Successful Communication in Life and at Work, The Berkley
Publishing Group, New York, New York, 2000,
ISBN 0-399-52614-5.

Lord, James Gregory, *A New Way of Looking at Organizations and
Philanthropy,* Appreciative Inquiry and the Quest,
copyright 2005 Philanthropic Quest International,
www.appreciative-inquiry.org./; info@lord.org;
Cleveland, Ohio.

Maxwell, John C., *Everyone Communicates, Few Connect:
What the Most Effective People Do Differently,* Thomas Nelson,
Nashville, 2010, ISBN 978-0-7852-1425-0.

MacDonald, George, Thinkexist.com.

McGinnis, Alan Loy, *The Friendship Factor,* Augsburg House
Publishing, Minneapolis, Minnesota, 1979, p. 22, 97.

McNally, David, *The Eagle's Secret: Success Strategies for Thriving
at Work & In Life,* Delacorte Press, New York, 1998, p. 143,
148, 176 ISBN 0-385-31427-2.

Melrose, Ken, *Making the Grass Greener on Your Side: A CEO's
Journey to Leading by Serving,* Berret-Koehler Publishers, Inc.
San Francisco, CA, 1995, p. 157, ISBN 1-881052-21-4.

Moss, Richard, in Lehman, *A Passion for the Game,* p. 63

Mother Teresa, in Maxwell, *Winning with People,* p. 248.

"Our Daily Bread," June/July 2010.

Peale, Norman Vincent, www.quotationspage.com.

Petrolino, Laura, Flying Pig Communications,
Flyingpigcommunications.com, Tampa, Florida.

Random Acts of Kindness, Conari Press (Editor), Berkely,
California, 1993.

Raiten-D'Antonio, Toni, *The Velveteen Principles: A Guide to
Becoming Real (Hidden Wisdom from a Children's Classic),*
Health Communications, Inc., Deerfield Beach, Florida, 2004,
ISBN 0-7573-0211-4.

Rilke, Rainer Maria, *Real Moments,* Dell, p. 174.

Russell, Armida, in *The Eagle's Secret: Success Strategies for
Thriving at Work & In Life,* Delacorte Press, New York, 1998,
p. 148, ISBN 0-385-31427-2.

Seligman, Martin E. P., *Authentic Happiness,* Free Press Division
of Simon and Schuster, New York, 2002.

Bibliography

Schweitzer, Albert, in Ken Melrose, *Making the Grass Greener on Your Side: A CEO's Journey to Leading by Serving,* Berret-Koehler Publishers, Inc. San Francisco, CA, 1995, p. 206, ISBN 1-881052-21-4.

Shea, Richard, editor, *The Book of Success,* Rutledge Hill Press, Nashville, TN, 1993, p.72, ISBN 1-55853-254-4.

Sheard, Jim and Armstrong, Wally, *Playing the Game: Inspiration for Life and Golf,* JCountryman, Nashville, Tennessee, 1998, ISBN 0-8499-5433-9.

Slim, Pamela, *Escape From Cubicle Nation,* EscapeFromCubicleNation.com.

Staubach, Roger, www.customerservicepoint.com/customer-service-quotes.html.

Steinberg, Leigh, brainyquote.com.

Tracey, Brian, *Create Your Own Future,* p. 119, 231, 232.

Trump, Donald at www.RicherSmarterHappier.com.

Walton, Sam, www.customerservicepoint.com/customer-service-quotes.html.

Warren, Rick, *The Purpose Driven Life,* Zondervan, Grand Rapids, Michigan, 2002, p. 131, ISBN 0-310-20571-9.

Washington, Booker T., in *Dungy.*

Williams, Margery, *The Velveteen Rabbit,* Alfred A Knopf, New York, 1990, ISBN 0-394-53221X.

Wooden, John, and Carty, Jay, *Coach Wooden's Pyramid of Success: Building Blocks for a Better Life,* Regal Books, Ventura, California, 2005, p. 43, ISBN 0-8307-3679-4.

Wordsworth, William, In McGinnis, Alan Loy, *The Friendship Factor,* Augsburg House Publishing, Minneapolis, Minnesota, 1979, p. 51.

York, Gary D. and Osness, Ken, *Master Strokes: Spiritual Growth through the Game of Golf,* Tyndale House Publishers, Inc., Wheaton, Illinois, 2000, , p. 30, 36, 48, 49, ISBN 0-8423-3592-7.

ABOUT THE AUTHORS

Larry Keltto is the founder and publisher of TheSolopreneurLife.com, which provides resources for solopreneurs. Larry has been a solopreneur since 1993; he specializes in providing marketing, communications, and coaching services to small businesses. He lives in Owatonna, Minnesota with his wife and two daughters.

Jim Sheard holds a doctorate degree in industrial psychology. Over the course of a 30-year career he has been a university professor, human resources consultant to organizations, and corporate president of Federated Insurance Companies.

He retired from business in 1996 and began writing and speaking. Jim is the co-author of six highly acclaimed gift books: *In His Grip,*

Playing the Game, A Champion's Heart, Finishing the Course, The Master's Grip, and *Fingerprints of Faith.* He recently self-published *Beyond the Score: Relationship Keys for Golf and Life.*

www.ingramcontent.com/pod-product-compliance
Lightning Source LLC
Chambersburg PA
CBHW022042190326
41520CB00008B/682